Who helps us?

In a supermarket

Vic Parker

Heinemann LIBRARY

Little Nippers

H **www.heinemann.co.uk/library**
Visit our website to find out more information about **Heinemann Library** books.

To order:
☎ Phone 44 (0) 1865 888066
📠 Send a fax to 44 (0) 1865 314091
💻 Visit the Heinemann Bookshop at www.heinemann.co.uk/library to browse our catalogue and order online.

First published in Great Britain by Heinemann Library, Halley Court, Jordan Hill, Oxford OX2 8EJ, part of Harcourt Education. Heinemann is a registered trademark of Harcourt Education Ltd.

Editorial: Jilly Attwood and Claire Throp
Design: Jo Hinton-Malivoire and bigtop, Bicester, UK
Models made by: Jo Brooker
Picture Research: Rosie Garai
Production: Séverine Ribierre

Originated by Dot Gradations
Printed and bound in China by South China Printing Company

ISBN 0 431 17323 0 (hardback)
08 07 06 05 04
10 9 8 7 6 5 4 3 2 1

ISBN 0 431 17328 1 (paperback)
08 07 06 05 04
10 9 8 7 6 5 4 3 2 1

British Library Cataloguing in Publication Data
Parker, Vic
In a supermarket – (Who helps us?)
381.1'48
A full catalogue record for this book is available from the British Library.

Acknowledgements
The publishers would like to thank the following for permission to reproduce photographs:
Peter Evans Photography pp. **4**, **5**, **7**, **9**, **11**, **12**, **13**, **14**, **15**, **16**, **17**, **18–19**, **21**, **22**, **23**; Trevor Hill p. **20**; Tudor Photography pp. **6**, **8**, **10**.

Cover photograph reproduced with permission of Peter Evans Photography.

The publishers would like to thank Annie Davy for her assistance in the preparation of this book.

Every effort has been made to contact copyright holders of any material reproduced in this book. Any omissions will be rectified in subsequent printings if notice is given to the publishers.

2

Contents

Behind closed doors

What happens when a supermarket is closed?

Busy cleaners keep it **bright** and **shiny**.

Taking deliveries

Drivers arrive.

Their trucks bring **big** boxes.

Workers open the boxes and fill the shelves, row by row by row.

Opening time

Here comes the manager.

Customer assistants

Who helps if you break something?

whoops!

Or if you can't find what you want?

customer assistant

Getting lost

If you get lost, what should you do?

Making a choice

Look at all the different cheeses.

What shape would you choose?

Deciding how much

Can you count the sausages?

At the checkout

Watch the shopping **slide** and **glide** along.

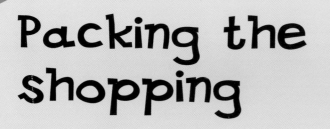

Packing the shopping

What a lot of shopping!

In the car park

Can you guess where this worker is taking the trolleys?

Index

The end

Notes for adults

The *Who helps us . . .?* series looks at a variety of people that a young child may come across in different situations. The books explore who these people are, why we might interact with them, and how to communicate appropriately. Used together, the books will enable discussion about similarities and differences between environments and people, and encourage the growth of the child's sense of self. The following Early Learning Goals are relevant to this series:

Knowledge and understanding of the world
Early learning goals for a sense of place:
• show an interest in the world in which they live
• notice differences between features of the local environment
• observe, find out about and identify features in the place they live and the natural world
• find out about their environment, and talk about those features they like and dislike.

Personal, social and emotional development
Early learning goals for a sense of community:
• make connections between different parts of their life experience
• understand that people have different needs, views, cultures and beliefs, which need to be treated with respect.
Early learning goals for self-confidence and self-esteem:
• separate from main carer with support/confidence

• express needs and feelings in appropriate ways
• initiate interactions with other people
• have a sense of self as a member of different communities
• respond to significant experiences, showing a range of feelings when appropriate
• have a developing awareness of their own needs, views and feelings and be sensitive to the needs, views and feelings of others.

This book introduces the reader to a range of people they may come across when at the supermarket. It will encourage young children to think about the jobs these people perform and how they help the community. **In a supermarket** will help children extend their vocabulary, as they will hear new words such as *deliveries* and *manager*. You may like to introduce and explain other new words yourself, such as *weighing scales* and *conveyor belt*.

Follow-up activities
• Make a list of the people in this book. On the next trip to the supermarket, see how many the child can spot and tick off on their list.
• Draw a picture of the inside of a supermarket, showing the workers doing their various jobs, and the child going shopping.
• Use role play to practise what a child should do if they get lost in a supermarket.